Cajun Home

Raymond Bial

Houghton Mifflin Company
Boston 1998

This book is respectfully dedicated to the Cajun people.

Acknowledgments

Cajuns are known for their generosity, and many people contributed to this book. I would like to thank the staff at the Acadian Village and at Vermilionville in Lafayette, Louisiana, for allowing me to photograph at their wonderful historic sites. Without the hard work of these people day in and day out, *Cajun Home* would not have been possible. I would also like to thank I. Bruce Turner, head of Archives and Special Collections at the University of Southwestern Louisiana, for supplying several fine photographs.

Among the many Cajun people I met along the way, I would like to extend special, heartfelt thanks to Dan Guillory, Gabrielle Boudreaux, Curtis Allemond, and Jimmy Guilbeau for their gracious help with this book.

I am grateful to Ann Rider for the opportunity to make *Cajun Home*, and to Anita Silvey, Kim Keller, Justin Barclay, and the other staff at Houghton Mifflin who have consistently supported my work. As always, I would like to thank my wife, Linda, and our children, Anna, Sarah, and Luke. Together we traveled to the bayous of Louisiana, where we met many friendly people, enjoyed too much good food, and happily danced a Cajun two-step.

Copyright © 1998 by Raymond Bial

The text of this book is set in Adobe Sabon.
Book design by Susan Sherman, Ars Agassiz, Cambridge, Massachusetts 02140-2244

Photo Credits
Pages 25, 32, and 42: courtesy University of Southwestern Louisiana Archives

Library of Congress Cataloging-in-Publication Data

Bial, Raymond.
Cajun home / written and with photographs by Raymond Bial.
p.   cm.
Summary: Discusses the history and culture of the Cajuns, French-speaking people who settled deep in the woods and bayous of Louisiana.
ISBN 0-395-86095-4
1. Cajuns—Louisiana—Social life and customs—Juvenile literature. 2. Louisiana—Social life and customs—Juvenile literature. 3. Cajuns—History—Juvenile literature. [1. Cajuns. 2. Louisiana—Social life and customs.] I. Title.
F380.A2B53   1998
976.3'004410763—dc21   97-20646   CIP   AC

Printed in Singapore
TWP 10 9 8 7 6 5 4 3 2 1

Parlez-vous Cajun?

Many Cajun words have been blended into the text, along with their definitions and pronunciation, to offer a little of the flavor of this unique culture and to acknowledge the rich heritage of the Cajun people. Children were once punished for speaking Cajun French in the schoolyard. Recently, an organization called CODOFIL (Council for the Development of French in Louisiana) was created to preserve this language, because if it is lost, so is the culture. Today at least thirteen Cajun dialects, which only faintly resemble modern French, are spoken in southern Louisiana. But to many people, Cajun French is the purest form of the language because it is "spoken from the heart."

Cajuns lived in modest frame houses, first in Acadia and later along the bayous in southern Louisiana. Many Cajuns still prefer a quiet life in the backcountry.

Deep in the woods and swamps of Louisiana live the Cajuns. These French-speaking people are known for their *joie de vivre* (JWAH de veev), or love of life, their rhythmic music, and their hot, spicy foods. A favorite saying among the Cajuns is "*Laissez le bon temps rouler*" (less-ay le bohn tahn roo-LAY), which means "Let the good times roll!" However, behind their ready smiles is a painful history, which began in France and continued when these hardy people migrated to North America, then later fled to southern Louisiana as exiles.

The Cajuns originally came from the northern coastal regions of France. Of independent spirit, they were mostly small farmers and artisans who resisted the injustices of the royal and religious authorities in the capital city of Paris. Having heard about the freedom of the New World, in 1632 they set sail across the stormy Atlantic Ocean for a colony established by the French explorer Samuel de Champlain in 1604. The land, now the Canadian Maritime Provinces of New Brunswick, Nova Scotia, and Prince Edward Island, was then called Acadia. That name may have been derived from the Greek word *arkadia,* meaning paradise, utopia, or land of dreams. Or the name may have come from *akade,* a word of the Micmac Indians who lived there, meaning "a place where things abound."

The name *Cajun* (KAY-jun) is a slang version of the word *Acadien,* which refers to the rural people who lived in that area of

Cajun society is based on close, loving families. This crib served as a bench during the day and was pushed against the parents' bed at night.

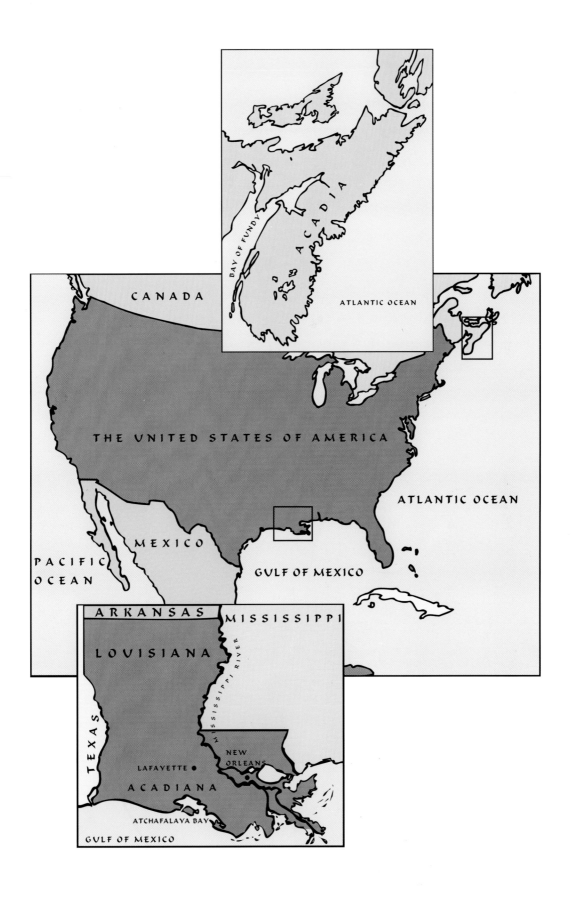

CANADA

ACADIA

BAY OF FUNDY

ATLANTIC OCEAN

THE UNITED STATES OF AMERICA

ATLANTIC OCEAN

MEXICO

PACIFIC
OCEAN

GULF OF MEXICO

ARKANSAS

MISSISSIPPI

LOUISIANA

MISSISSIPPI RIVER

TEXAS

NEW
ORLEANS

LAFAYETTE

ACADIANA

ATCHAFALAYA BAY

GULF OF MEXICO

Canada. The Acadians, as the Cajuns were first called, made homes for themselves as farmers and fishermen near Port Royal on the Bay of Fundy, where they learned to build dikes to control the high tides that washed over the low coastal lands. As the settlement grew to about 18,000 inhabitants, their sense of loyalty as a group was strengthened, and they established a deep feeling for the land.

Over the next hundred years, the Acadians proved to be quite resourceful and resilient in reinventing themselves as a people. Poor and persecuted in France, they broke from the Old World

Since the time they lived in France over three hundred years ago, Cajuns have been highly skilled with their hands. In North America this sturdy wheelbarrow was useful for carrying materials around the farm or workshop.

Having to provide for themselves in the wilderness of North America, early Cajuns made baskets and long wooden bowls for making French bread and other foods in the kitchen.

and fashioned a distinctive French-Canadian culture. They continued to speak French and maintained some of their earlier customs and trades as shipbuilders, blacksmiths, and carpenters. Yet, like the French explorers and traders called *coureurs de bois* (coo-rur de BWAH), they also learned from the Indians to gather native plants such as wild carrots and cranberries, to hunt in the woods, and to find oysters, clams, and lobsters along the saltwater coast. They became skilled at making snowshoes, birchbark canoes, and other goods necessary to their survival in the North American wilderness.

Unconcerned about maintaining a purely French heritage, the Acadians intermarried with the Micmacs and had children who came to be called *métis* (may-TEE), which means half-breed. They absorbed others of European descent into their ever-changing, dynamic society as well. A family of Scottish settlers not only joined the Acadian community and spoke their language, but changed the spelling of their name to Melonson so they would seem more French. All these ethnic groups became part of the blend of languages, customs, and traditions that grew into a unique Acadian culture.

Distrustful of authority, the Acadians didn't care for politics and government. They simply wished to live peacefully in their homes between the coastal waters and the forest, cultivating the land, fishing in the ocean, and working at various trades. However, Acadia was claimed both by the British, when John Cabot discovered it in 1497, and by the French, who colonized the area in the early 1600s. Unfortunately, the Acadians found themselves caught between two European powers battling for supremacy in the New World. They had been living in their colony for several generations when it was formally ceded to Great Britain in 1713 in the Treaty of Utrecht.

The Acadians tried to remain neutral, but because they spoke French, they were looked upon with suspicion. They suffered terribly at the hands of brutal British commanders, notably Major Charles Lawrence, who was described by one of his own men as a "low, crafty tyrant and accomplished flatterer." In 1755, during the conflict between France and Great Britain known in North America as the French and Indian War, the British decided to expel those Catholic inhabitants who wouldn't swear allegiance to

In Louisiana, the Cajuns were driven deep into the Atchafalaya Swamp. The largest wetland in North America, the Atchafalya teems with fish, alligators, crawfish, and other wildlife. It is the heart of Cajun country.

the Crown. The Acadian families were torn apart and, with few clothes and little food, were jammed into the cargo holds of creaky wooden ships. Sent away from their homes in the bitter winter, one in three people fell ill, starved, or froze to death during the turbulent journey. About 6,000 survivors were scattered throughout the American colonies from New England to the Carolinas, where they were forced to labor as indentured servants, and the West Indies. This description of their plight came to be known as *le grand dérangement* (le grahn DAY-rahngemahn), which means the great dispersal or scattering. Henry Wadsworth

In Longfellow's poem, Evangeline's lover waits faithfully beneath a spreading oak tree in St. Martinsville, Louisiana, but, sadly, the young woman does not find him until many years later, when he is on his deathbed.

Longfellow recounted their anguish in his long narrative poem, *Evangeline.*

Several hundred Acadian refugees eventually found their way to the backwaters of Louisiana, where they struggled to make homes on the low, swampy ground at the mouth of the Mississippi River.

Between 1765 and 1785 they were joined by other Acadians who had been banished from Canada. Together the Acadians managed to build a community for themselves near the cities of New Orleans and Lafayette. Yet even after their arrival in Louisiana, they encountered persecution. The United States acquired the land on which they lived from France in the Louisiana Purchase of 1803, and Louisiana became a state in 1812. In a second exile, many Cajuns were forced off the better, more fertile land by the Americans and driven deep into the swamps and marshes and onto the prairie across a large swamp called Atchafalaya Bay.

Many Cajuns built their homes near the water. With bayous serving as roads, they could conveniently travel by boat to nearby villages to purchase coffee, sugar, flour, and other provisions, as well as to sell produce from their gardens.

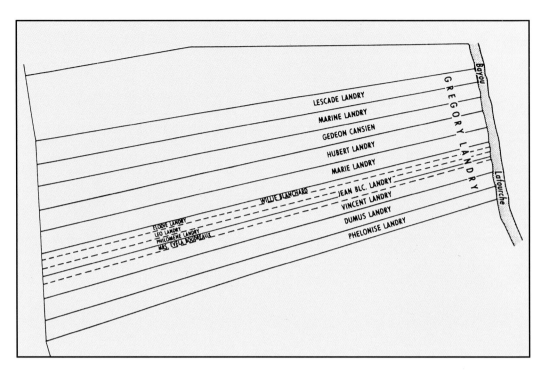

Early Cajuns carried on some French traditions. The division of the land in these ribbon farms appears unusual, but each farm provided its owner with a variety of land types—fields, woods, and frontage on the bayou.

Water travel and inheritance laws helped to create a unique system of land division in Cajun country. "Line villages," similar to those in Acadia, were established along the natural levees, or high banks, of the slow-flowing streams called bayous (BY-yous). The bayous served as roads and highways because boats were the only means of transporting people and goods in such swampy country. The first Acadians to settle on the low ground established ribbon farms along the bayous. These long, narrow strips of land each had some frontage on the bayou, to ensure access to the water for fishing and travel by boat, and a varied terrain extending back from the water—fields for farming, woods for hunting

The swamp provided many resources, including cypress wood. Because it never decayed, cypress was used for making homes and fences, as well as buckets, tubs, and washboards.

Living in low country, people couldn't always be assured of safe drinking water, so they made large barrels, called cisterns, from cypress wood. Placed next to the house, the cistern collected fresh rainwater.

and collecting firewood, and marshes for trapping. The Acadians followed French inheritance laws, which required equal division of property among the children, so the ribbon farms became very slender as they were repeatedly divided over the years.

Early Cajuns harvested trees, especially cypress, tupelo gum, red maple, ash, and willow, to build homes for their families. The most common kind of house came to be a small one-and-a-half-story frame cottage raised on pillars or blocks to keep the sill off the soggy ground. The four rooms were often separated by a central hall with fireplaces on each side but with just one chimney. Since marsh water often wasn't fit to drink, many homes had drainpipes and cisterns to collect rainwater for the household. A front porch, called a *galerie* (gal-air-EE), was built into the frame of the house. The porch was an ideal place to sit on summer days, drinking dark-roasted coffee while visiting with family and friends. On especially hot nights, the family often slept out on the porch.

As *petits habitants* (peh-TEET ah-bee-TAHN), small yeoman farmers and craftspeople, Cajuns rejected the American emphasis upon factories and industry, preferring to live off the land. Along with raising cotton, corn, and cattle, they hunted alligators, turtles, frogs, and crawfish in the swamps for food and cash income.

Both lovely and useful, this pirogue is an example of fine Cajun craftsmanship. With graceful lines and a flat bottom, the boat floated lightly over the shallow water of the bayous.

Cajuns have always loved to get out on the water to catch fish, trap muskrats, and hunt alligators. Among their many practical crafts was the carving of wooden decoys, used to attract ducks into landing in the swamp.

According to an old saying, "If it walks, crawls, swims, or flies, it ends up in the Cajun's pot." They caught shrimp and fish in the Gulf of Mexico and freshwater fish in the inland waters. They trapped and sold the fur pelts of beaver, mink, otter, raccoon, muskrat, and later nutria, a South American rodent resembling a large muskrat that was introduced into the region. To get around their watery communities, they used a variety of shallow-bottomed boats that were either paddled or poled, including the *pirogue* (PEE-rohg), a long, slender version of the Native American dugout. They also invented a wide, flat-bottomed boat, or *bateau* (bah-TOH), that was not easily capsized and the *joug* (joog), a kind of skiff that was rowed from a standing position.

Cajun women often gathered to sew patchwork quilts of homespun, hand-woven cotten. First they grew the cotton, both white and brown, which they referred to as jaune *or* yellow cotton.

Highly skilled weavers, Cajun women not only made the clothing for their families but wove all the household cloth goods.

Many Cajuns earned a living as craftspeople. They were not only skilled at building a variety of boats, but were talented in blacksmithing, carpentry, pottery, and other crafts. Some items that they used as musical instruments, such as washboards and spoons, could be found around the house, but self-taught artisans made others, notably fiddles, accordions, and guitars, or repaired vintage instruments. Women sewed clothes for their families, sometimes from purchased calico cloth, but usually they spun their own cotton and wool into thread, then wove it into cloth. They were expert weavers of rugs, curtains, tablecloths, bed sheets, and blankets. From the Indians, Cajuns also learned to

Early Cajun clothing was commonly made from distinctive striped fabric, as shown in the skirt and shirt. Later, they began to wear store-bought calico and denim.

An artisan made these beautifully shaped wooden shoes, or sabots, *which were worn by early Cajun people. The shoes were well suited to the low, swampy ground of southern Louisiana.*

weave dried leaves and grasses into fans, pine needle baskets, and palmetto hats.

Living in relative isolation from their English-speaking neighbors, the Cajuns remained unchanged through most of the nineteenth century. They grew white and "yellow" cotton in small fields and raised sheep for wool in their meadows. They preferred to wear cotton clothing in the warm, humid climate of Louisiana, where summer temperatures soared into the nineties. Men typically wore knee-length pants called *braguettes* (brah-GET), cottonade or homespun shirts, and jackets, along with hand-woven palmetto hats. Women preferred boldly striped dresses in bright colors—

yellow, red, violet, and purple—along with gray or white stockings. The bodice was usually made of a different fabric and dyed bright red. The outfit was complemented with a striped or brightly colored kerchief or, more often, a *gardesoleil* (gar-de-so-LAY), or sun bonnet, and a *barbé* (bar-BAY), a shoulder-length sunshade. Before the Civil War, young boys and girls wore dresses fastened with a clasp at the back, then later dressed like their parents. Children generally went barefoot until they were at least ten years old. They then wore moccasins called *savates* (sah-VAHT), or slippers. Some Cajuns also made and wore wooden shoes, or *sabots* (sah-BO), which literally means hoofs as well as any large, clumsy shoes, but most often they wore moccasins, at least until the end of the nineteenth century when women began to spend their egg money on factory-made shoes, called *souliers*.

The family was a primary influence in maintaining Cajun culture, and mothers played an especially important role in emphasizing family unity in the face of many challenges—death at the hands of British authorities, families broken apart by exile and scattered across the continent, as well as discrimination in Louisiana. Fathers were warm and loving with their children and often joked with them. There were many more Irish, German, and other ethnic groups in Louisiana than the Cajuns themselves. Though usually poorer than these people and sometimes involved in conflict with them, Cajuns often absorbed them into *their* culture with its distinctive French flavor. They had large extended families, and they loved to socialize with relatives and friends, so other people simply found it more enjoyable to become Cajun.

Living in the backcountry, Cajuns didn't have radios or even local newspapers. So the family would hang a quilt on the porch railing to let passersby know they had news of a marriage or death.

Everyone in the Cajun community loved to get together frequently to "pass a good time." As one old grandmother explained, "Our manner of living in Acadia was peculiar, the people forming, as it were, one single family." Like other rural people, Cajuns socialized at church and other events for work and fun, and there was always plenty of good food, dancing, music, storytelling, and games. During the harvest season, they often participated in a *ramasserie* (rah-mah-ser-EE), or communal harvest, in which families came together to help with the arduous tasks of picking cotton or corn. If someone needed help, a special kind of cooperative work effort, the *coups de main* (coo de man), which literally means "strokes of the hand," was called for. If a farmer was sick or injured, his neighbors gathered at his home and brought in his crops for him, usually in a single day. Cajun folks also got together for *boucheries* (boo-share-EE), or country butcherings, in which hogs were slaughtered and the meat shared among the families. Laughing and gossiping, everyone pitched in and made spicy sausages called *boudin* (BOO-dan), cracklings or *gratons* (grah-

These Cajun women are working at a boucherie, *or hog butchering. Many people came together for hard work and a good time. At the end of the day, they shared the meat.*

TONE), and smoked hams. Like other country people, Cajuns were frugal, using every part of the pig except the squeal.

Community life was also strengthened by the popular dances called *bals de maison* (bahl de may-SOHN). Held in different family homes, *bals de maison* helped preserve traditional music, dance, language, and cooking. They also provided opportunities for young men and women to court under the careful supervision of parents and older brothers and sisters. Later in the nineteenth century, the *bals* gradually moved to public dance halls. Yet Cajun dances remained family events, and the children were always

Cajun girls slept downstairs and were closely supervised. On hot, humid nights the family spread mosquito netting over their beds.

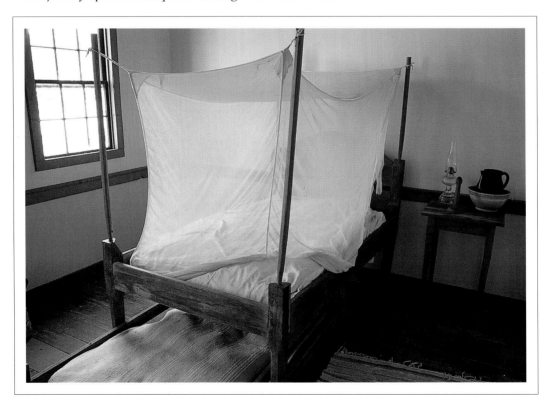

Sleeping upstairs, Cajun boys generally came and went as they pleased, using the stairs on the galerie.

brought along. If the young ones got tired, they could sleep in a bed in a room called the *parc aux petits* (park oh peh-TEE), which means pen or enclosure for the little ones. Today the *fais-dodo* (FAY-dough-dough) is a popular country dance, named for the custom of rocking children to sleep in a room next to the dance hall. Families also got together, especially in the quiet of winter, for evening visits or *veillées* (vay-YAY), at which they enjoyed coffee, desserts, and lots of talk, often enlivened with storytelling and singing. When everyone ended up speaking at once, the Cajuns called it *gumbo ya-ya*. Radio, and later television, changed but did not destroy this custom.

The Catholic Church also helped strengthen Cajun culture. Although they disliked authority, Cajuns had deep, heartfelt religious beliefs, going back to their years of poverty in France. Weddings and funerals were benchmark times in people's lives, when everyone gathered under the roof of a country church, either to celebrate a marriage or mourn the death of a loved one.

There were many special funeral customs among the Cajun people. Clocks were stopped at the time of death, and no work was done. The wake, or visitation, was usually held in the home of the deceased person, whose body was laid out in one of the rooms. If the person had been old, the coffin was shrouded, or draped, in black cloth; for a young person, it was covered in white. Two candles lighted the body, whose feet always faced the door, to allow the deceased person to travel to the other world. Friends and family paid their respects, then met in another room to talk among themselves. After the wake, someone stayed in the house, because the body was not supposed to be left alone before burial. Along the route to the cemetery, people closed their shutters and doors to keep out any wandering spirits. Such superstitions were very much a part of Cajun life. For example, alligator teeth and oil were used for home remedies, but if an alligator was seen crawling under the house, it was a portent, or sign, of death.

Cajun courtships were very structured; the young man visited the parents and occasionally saw their daughter, but always with a chaperone. After several visits, he might ask the parents for the young woman's hand in marriage, on a Thursday. If she and the parents agreed, the couple got a marriage license on Saturday, and

Although they remain suspicious of organized religion, Cajuns have traditionally looked to their deeply held faith as a source of strength and unity.

the wedding announcement, or banns, was made at church on the following three Sundays. The marriage was then held on the next Saturday. One wedding tradition was that the bride and her family walked around the dance floor to the tune of the *marche des mariés* (marsh day mah-ree-AY). The bride and groom then danced a waltz and asked the others to join the wedding dance.

Whenever people got together there was plenty of good food. Meals have always been an important part of Cajun life—not simply for sustenance but as an art form. Except for store-bought flour, early Cajuns provided for themselves, growing their own vegetables, raising their own livestock, or hunting and gathering seafood, fish, game, and whatever else went into the cooking pot. Many early dishes were similar to typical pioneer fare—corn-

---

JAMBALAYA (*jum-bah-LIE-ah*)

Seasoned with herbs, jambalaya is made with rice and various other ingredients, including sausage. There are many ways to make this dish; this recipe is adapted from a favorite at Vermilionville in Lafayette, Louisiana. You may substitute *boudin* or other spicy sausage for the pork ribs, or add other ingredients, such as ham, chicken, shrimp, or oysters.

1 medium onion	salt and pepper
1 bell pepper	2–3 lbs. pork ribs cut in 2-inch lengths
1 stalk celery, chopped	2 cans tomatoes
1 green onion, chopped	3 ½ cups rice
1 tablespoon garlic	5–6 dashes Tabasco sauce
½ stick butter	3 ½ cups water

1. Lightly season the rib meat with salt and pepper, then brown in a large pot. Add a little water to make a gravy. Set aside.
2. Melt the butter in the pot and sauté onion, bell pepper, and celery.
3. Add canned tomatoes, uncooked rice, water, ribs, and green onion to the sautéed mixture.
4. Bring to a boil, cover, and cook over low heat 30–40 minutes or until the rice is tender.
5. Remove from heat, set aside for five minutes, and serve.

Ça c'est bon! (That's good!)

Early Cajuns ate the same foods as other country people in Louisiana, such as this field-pea soup, but they added their own ingredients and flavors to traditional recipes, including crawfish, which turn vivid red when boiled.

bread, potatoes, beans, and meat—but French-Canadian heritage and the swampy geography of southern Louisiana resulted in some unique features, such as the generous use of peppers and hot spices. Like their ancestors in Acadia, the Cajuns relied on boiling, a cooking method well suited to the foods of Louisiana, to make stews such as gumbo, a favorite dish.

It is said that Cajuns do not eat to live but live to eat, especially among family and friends. Holidays (such as Christmas, New Year's, and Mardi Gras), the seasons, and the weather determine

Living off the land, Cajuns once ate crawfish and other wild foods out of necessity. Today large crowds often gather at crawfish boils. A huge pot is used to cook the small creatures.

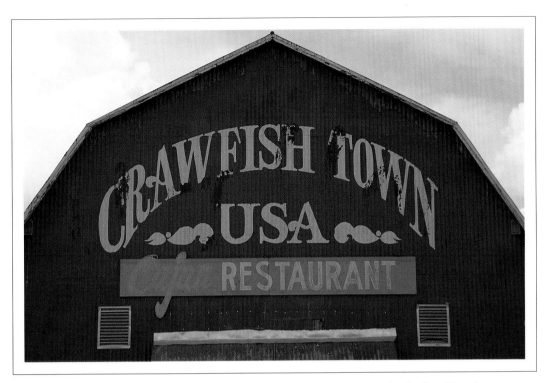

Today good restaurants abound in Cajun country, most of which offer their own special recipes for crawfish along with jambalaya and gumbo. Crawfish are most often boiled with spices or cooked in a rich sauce called an étouffée.

the nature of their social events. Crawfish, crab, and shrimp boils are held outdoors in the spring and summer, and the men do the cooking under a shade tree. Crawfish, or *écrevisses* (AY-creh-VEESE), are so popular that Cajuns have learned to raise the little crustaceans in earthen ponds during the cool winter months. (During the warm months rice is sometimes grown in the same ponds.) It is said that the lobster loved the Cajun people so much that it followed them from Acadia to Louisiana. On the way, it repeatedly molted, or shed its skin, getting smaller and smaller, until it became the feisty little crawfish.

Over the years, Cajuns have continued to intermarry with other

Many Cajuns still prefer to make their homes back in the swamps, where they live off the land—and the water—by hunting, fishing, and trapping.

ethnic groups and are now a blend of French, African, and Native American heritages, along with many others. Today there are blue-eyed Cajuns with red or blond hair. Many French-speaking Cajuns have German, Spanish, or Scottish names. More than fifteen ethnic groups are represented in the culture, including Filipino and Lebanese. Still, the most common family names—such as Broussard, Boudreaux, Guillory, and Thibaut—have strong French roots.

Cajun culture is similar to gumbo. Taking its name from the African word *gombo,* the dish is based on French cuisine, but it includes local game and seafood. Like African and Native American dishes, it is thickened and flavored with African okra or

*Fluent in English and the Cajun dialect of French, Curtis
Allemond is Cajun through and through, and he has the name
to prove it. Yet other Cajuns have Scotch and Irish roots.*

Native American *filé* (FEE-lay)—powdered sassafras leaves—and seasoned with hot spices from the Caribbean. Rice also became an important ingredient in Cajun cooking as it became *créole* (CRAY-ole), or "home-grown, not imported." The term originally referred to French people born in Louisiana, then to people and things native to the state. Now the word *créole* is most often used to describe French-speaking African Americans in Louisiana. Creoles have intermarried with Cajuns and share their ancestry and culture, particularly in language and music.

Cajun songs range from seventeenth-century French ballads to familiar southern country tunes sung with French lyrics. Cajun music blends a strong French folk tradition with American Indian, Scotch-Irish, Spanish, German, Anglo-American, and Afro-Caribbean elements to create a zesty type of country and blues music. Dewey Balfa, a highly respected Cajun folk musician, recalled, "My father, grandfather, great-grandfather, they all played the fiddle, and, you see, through my music, I feel they are all still alive."

Since the 1920s Cajun music has made its way onto records and the radio, becoming popular throughout the nation. It has influenced well-known musicians such as Hank Williams, who wrote and sang tunes, including "Jambalaya," that were popular in the rural dance halls known as honky-tonks. Today Cajuns have become particularly well known for their unique style of music sung in French. A kind of Creole music called zydeco (ZIE-deh-co) has also become popular. A blend of French lyrics and Africanized rhythms, zydeco is usually played by a band consisting

Talented musicians like Curley Leger, Aldus Rogers (pronounced all-DOO roe-JZAY), *and Less Credeur play the fiddle, accordion, and guitar. At get-togethers, old and young alike dance the two-step to a* chanky-chank *beat.*

of an accordion, a guitar, and a washboard.

Over the years, stereotypes emerged about the Cajuns, who were considered coarse people who lived in woods and swamps thick with alligators and snakes. As recently as 1939, writing for the Federal Writers' Project, Marguerite A. Pecot described Cajun men as "robust, sinewy, with heavily tanned skin, coarse irregular features, dark bushy hair, and dull, rather unimaginative eyes; the women during adolescence and girlhood possess a certain youthful charm, but four or five years of connubial felicity unfailingly take the glow from their eyes and the delicate flush from their cheeks."

Pecot further unfairly described Cajuns as uneducated, emotional, and lacking stability in their lives. Her words are both inaccurate and hurtful; Cajuns are delightful people known for their hard work and generosity.

Cajuns did not begin to "Americanize" until the early years of this century. With the discovery of oil in 1901, more outsiders came into the backcountry of Louisiana, and Cajuns left their farms to take jobs in the refineries. With the passage of the Education Act of 1916, all children were required to attend school, where only English was spoken. During World War I, nationalism became more important in the United States, and President Theodore Roosevelt called for "one country, one language." As in the rest of rural America, the automobile, radio, and telephone brought Cajuns into contact with other parts of the country.

Still, a visit to Cajun country today is like going back in time, at least to the 1950s, to lonesome roadside cafés, grocery stores, and old gas stations. The roads from New Orleans stretch over the Atchafalaya Swamp into what Cajuns call "the prairie." Weathered barns have painted signs advertising soda pop in French. Many Cajuns still live in small, tightly knit rural communities in the bayous and backwoods. They still like to hunt, fish, and trap. They also practice traditional crafts, such as spinning and weaving in their homes, or are reviving their unique customs, yet they may now make a *roux* (roo) in a microwave.

Today Cajuns speak their own *patois* (pa-TWAH), or dialect, of archaic French enriched with Spanish, English, German, African, and Native American words. For instance, the Cajun word for

*An Acadian flag adorns this classroom today, but Cajun children were once for-
bidden to speak their French dialect on school grounds. Persisting on the banks
of the bayous, they have struggled to keep their language and culture alive.*

One stereotype is that Cajuns love dancing and food, but there is more to the culture than chanky-chank *and good eating. Most people still prefer a quiet life at home in the country.*

bullfrog is not the French *grenouille* (grahn-WEEH) but the Huron and Iroquois word *ouaouaron* (oowah-oowah-ROHN). The familiar word *bayou* comes from the Choctaw language. Cajuns still practice their own distinctive version of the Roman Catholic religion. A complex people, Cajuns are easygoing yet stubborn; friendly yet suspicious of strangers; deeply religious yet disdainful of established church rules; loyal yet fiercely independent; proud yet quick to laugh at their own mistakes. There is a local joke: "You can tell a Cajun a mile away, but you can't tell him a damn thing up close." Yet their common suffering—at the hands of aristocrats and priests in France, the English governors in

Acadia, and *les Américains* (lays ah-MARE-i-can) in Louisiana—has fostered a powerful and enduring sense of group loyalty.

Mardi Gras (MAR-dee grah), which literally means "Fat Tuesday," is the most famous event in Louisiana. It is jubilantly celebrated with parades and parties in which the participants dress in wild costumes, usually in gold, purple, and green. Held in February or March on the day before Ash Wednesday, Mardi Gras is the last chance to eat, drink, and dance before the forty days of sacrifice during Lent. The rural Cajun and black Creole *courir de Mardi Gras* (coo-reer de MAR-dee grah) features a group of rev-

Swathed in green foliage and overhung with tree branches, bayous flow so slowly the water appears to be standing still. Over the past 250 years this land has come to be home to thousands of Cajun people.

Dressed up for Mardi Gras, this couple pauses in their journey through the countryside beside their pony and buggy. Part of the fun of Mardi Gras is trying to guess the identity of the costumed people.

elers dressed as clowns, thieves, devils, and women who visit houses on horseback in Mamou and other prairie towns. Led by a *capitaine* (ca-pee-TAN), who keeps order, they demand *charité* (shah-ree-TAY), in the form of a live chicken, rice, sausages, spices, or other ingredients for a large gumbo supper. At each house the *capitaine* asks, *"Voulez-vous recevoir cette bande de Mardi Gras?"* ("Do you want to receive this Mardi Gras band?") After dismounting and dancing in the yard, the men chase down a live chicken that has been tossed in the air. When caught and killed, the chicken becomes part of the spoils for the cooking pot, to be taken back to the "hub," or headquarters, in town. When they leave the house, the men sing the Mardi Gras song, which traces its history to medieval French folk music.

Cajun people still appreciate both hard work and *bon temps,* as well as a generous spirit, because giving remains at the heart of their lives. Cajuns have very much enriched American culture, not only with Saturday night dances featuring jukeboxes or live fiddle music, and good cooking, but with their dignified struggle to preserve their way of life. Today there are nearly one million Cajuns

Many Cajun people still enjoy getting away to the backwaters of the Atchafalaya Swamp. They may spend a few days, weeks, or all summer living on their houseboats among the cypress trees.

Cajun country, which is also called Acadiana, has become a popular tourist attraction, and for good reason. The region offers delicious food, including boudin, *a spicy sausage that has long been a local favorite.*

living in Acadiana, which includes roughly the lower third of the state of Louisiana. With the city of Lafayette in the cultural and geographic center, the region stretches from the coast across Atchafalaya Bay to the prairies and includes fishing villages on the Gulf of Mexico and little farms back in the swamps of black water and Spanish moss. Both enchanted and earthy, it's a place where everyone is welcome to come visit and "pass a good time."

Further Reading

Many excellent books are available in libraries and bookstores for those who would like to learn more about Cajun history and culture. *Cajun Country* is an especially fine book that I found very helpful in understanding these wonderful people. Along with visiting southern Louisiana and talking with many friendly people about the Cajun way of life, I consulted the following sources which will be of value to anyone wishing to learn more about the Cajuns.

Ancelet, Barry Jean, Jay D. Edwards, and Glen Pitre. *Cajun Country.* Jackson: University Press of Mississippi, 1991.

Ancelet, Barry Jean. *Cajun and Creole Folktales: The French Oral Tradition of Southern Louisiana.* New York: Garland, 1994.

Angers, Trent. *The Truth about the Cajuns.* Lafayette, La.: Acadian House Publishing, 1989.

Brasseaux, Carl A. *Acadian to Cajun: Transformation of a People, 1803–1877.* Jackson: University Press of Mississippi, 1992.

Comeau, Malcolm L. *Atchafalaya Swamp Life: Settlement and Folk Occupations.* Baton Rouge: Louisiana State University School of Geoscience, 1972.

Conrad, Glenn R., ed. *The Cajuns: Essays on Their History and Culture,* 2nd ed. Lafayette, La.: University of Southwestern Louisiana Center for Louisiana Studies, 1978.

Daigle, Jules O. *A Dictionary of the Cajun Language*. Ann Arbor, Mich.: Edwards Brothers, 1984.

Deffes, Joe. *People of the Bayou: Cajun Life in Lost America*. New York: E. P. Dutton, 1979.

Dorman, James H. *The People Called Cajuns: An Introduction to an Ethnohistory*. Lafayette, La.: University of Southwestern Louisiana Center for Louisiana Studies, 1983.

Gould, Philip. *Cajun Music and Zydeco*. Baton Rouge: Louisiana State University Press, 1992.

Gutierrez, C. Paige. *Cajun Foodways*. Jackson: University Press of Mississippi, 1992.

Newton, Milton B., Jr. *Atlas of Louisiana: A Guide for Students*. Baton Rouge: Louisiana State University School of Geoscience, 1992.

Rushton, William Faulkner. *The Cajuns: From Acadia to Louisiana*. New York: Farrar, Straus, and Giroux, 1979.

Saxon, Lyle. *Gumbo Ya-Ya: A Collection of Louisiana Folk Tales*. New York: Bonanza Books, 1945.

Wilson, Charles Reagan, and William Ferris, eds. *Encyclopedia of Southern Culture*. Chapel Hill: University of North Carolina Press, 1989.

Young readers may especially enjoy the following books:

Hoyt-Goldsmith, Diane, with photographs by Lawrence Migdale. *Mardi Gras: A Cajun Country Celebration*. New York: Holiday House, 1995.

Reneaux, J. J. *Cajun Folktales*. Little Rock, Ark.: August House Publishers, 1992.

Thomassie, Tynia, with illustrations by Cat Bowman Smith. *Feliciana Feydra le Roux*. Boston: Little, Brown, 1995.

9/3/99